Helping the Environment

Using Less Water

by Nick Rebman

FOCUS READERS.

BEACON

www.focusreaders.com

Focus Readers is distributed by North Star Editions:
sales@northstareditions.com | 888-417-0195

Produced for Focus Readers by Red Line Editorial.

Photographs ©: iStockphoto, cover, 1, 29; Shutterstock Images, 4, 6, 8, 11, 13, 14, 17, 19, 20–21, 22, 25; Jacquelyn Martin/AP Images, 27

Library of Congress Cataloging-in-Publication Data
Names: Rebman, Nick, author.
Title: Using less water / by Nick Rebman.
Description: Lake Elmo : Focus Readers, [2022] | Series: Helping the environment | Includes index. | Audience: Grades 2-3
Identifiers: LCCN 2021012453 (print) | LCCN 2021012454 (ebook) | ISBN 9781644938409 (hardcover) | ISBN 9781644938867 (paperback) | ISBN 9781644939321 (ebook) | ISBN 9781644939758 (pdf)
Subjects: LCSH: Water consumption--Juvenile literature. | Sustainable living--Juvenile literature.
Classification: LCC TD348 .R43 2022 (print) | LCC TD348 (ebook) | DDC 363.6/1--dc23
LC record available at https://lccn.loc.gov/2021012453
LC ebook record available at https://lccn.loc.gov/2021012454

Printed in the United States of America
Mankato, MN
082021

About the Author

Nick Rebman enjoys reading, drawing, and taking long walks with his dog. He lives in Minnesota.

Table of Contents

CHAPTER 1

Fixing a Sink 5

CHAPTER 2

Wasting Water 9

CHAPTER 3

Working on Solutions 15

THAT'S AMAZING!

Aerators 20

CHAPTER 4

How to Help 23

Focus on Using Less Water • 28
Glossary • 30
To Learn More • 31
Index • 32

Fixing a Sink

A boy wakes up on Saturday morning. First, he takes a quick shower. Then, he puts on his favorite jeans. He also puts on an old shirt. The boy has had these clothes for a long time.

 The average shower takes eight minutes and uses 17 gallons (64 L) of water.

 Simple tools such as wrenches can help fix many leaks.

The boy eats oatmeal and a banana for breakfast. He finishes every bite. When he is done, he puts his bowl in the dishwasher.

Next, the boy and his mom get out their tool set. The bathroom sink is leaking. So, they fix it. Now the sink doesn't drip anymore.

Fixing a leaky sink is a great way to save water. So is taking a short shower. But these were not the only ways the boy reduced water waste. All of his actions this morning were helpful. That's because producing food and clothing uses water, too.

Did You Know?

Newer dishwashers use far less water than washing dishes by hand.

Chapter 2

Wasting Water

Everyone needs water to live. But many people are wasteful with water. For example, some homes have leaky faucets. Many people take long showers. Others keep the tap on while they wash dishes.

 In one year, a leaky sink can waste 3,000 gallons (11,400 L) of water.

Also, people often use sprinklers to water their lawns.

However, there is an even bigger problem. Most water is used outside the home. In particular, farms use huge amounts of water. Farmers often use sprinklers to water crops. But these sprinklers

Did You Know?

Making energy from fossil fuels such as coal requires lots of water. Energy made from the sun and wind uses much less.

 Watering crops with tools such as sprinklers is known as irrigation.

tend to be very wasteful. Much of the water **evaporates** before it reaches the soil. Even if the water does reach the soil, it may not go to the crops' roots.

Raising animals takes far more water than growing crops. That's because animals eat tons of food. All of that food needs water to grow.

Factories use lots of water, too. Clothing, metal, and paper are all made using water. In fact, water is needed to make nearly everything that people buy.

Wasting water can lead to major problems. Over time, water **sources** can dry up. That can lead to **droughts**. And droughts

▷ Between 2000 and 2020, parts of Africa and Asia were especially hard-hit by droughts.

make it harder to grow crops.

This problem does not affect all

countries equally. It tends to affect

low-income countries the most.

Chapter 3

Working on Solutions

Designers wanted to reduce water waste in homes. So, they came up with better toilets. These toilets use less water for each flush. Designers made new faucets, too. They use less water per minute.

 In most homes, more than half of all water is used in the bathroom.

Outside the home, some people have gotten rid of their lawns. Instead, they grow **native** plants. These plants can usually survive without being watered. So, there is no need for wasteful sprinklers.

Farmers are also reducing water waste. Many farmers have pipes in their fields. These pipes send

Did You Know?

Farms use approximately 70 percent of Earth's fresh water.

 Drip irrigation helps lettuce crops grow.

drips of water to the roots of crops.
This system uses much less water
than sprinklers. Other farmers have
started growing different crops.
They choose crops that need
less water.

Many factories are reusing water. For example, they may need some water for cleaning. They may also need water to keep machines cool. That's because machines can get very hot. Factories save their cleaning water. Then they reuse that water to cool their machines.

Cities are helping, too. Some cities are planting rain gardens. Rainwater flows into these gardens. Then the water soaks into the ground. That increases the supply

Creating rain gardens is one of many ways cities can protect fresh water.

of groundwater. It also cuts down

on **runoff**. So, lakes and rivers

become less polluted. Those

freshwater sources are protected.

Aerators

Aerators are small devices that make faucets use less water. They do not cost much. Even so, many faucets do not have them.

A student in Bengaluru, India, wanted to change that. He spoke to the **manager** of a hotel. The manager agreed to put an aerator in every faucet. After one year, the hotel had saved 1.3 million gallons (5 million L) of water.

The student also spoke to the principal of his school. She agreed to start using aerators, too. The student showed that one person can make a big difference.

Using aerators is an easy way to save water.

Chapter 4

How to Help

There are many ways you can help reduce water waste. At home, you can avoid taking baths. Instead, take short showers. You can even put a timer in the bathroom. Try to keep showers under five minutes.

 The average bath uses nearly twice as much water as the average shower.

Turn off the water while you brush your teeth. When you do the dishes, fill the sink rather than leaving the water on. Also, fix any leaks.

The grocery store is a great place to reduce water waste. Try to buy more plant-based foods. These foods use much less water than

Did You Know?

Some people have rain barrels outside their homes. These barrels collect rainwater. Then the water can be used for gardens.

 It takes approximately 650 gallons (2,460 L) of water to make one cotton T-shirt.

meat. Buy only what you need. When you waste food, you also waste the water that helped grow it.

In addition, you can reduce your water waste when you buy clothes.

Factories use large amounts of water when they make clothing. So, be sure to buy clothes that will last a long time. That way, you won't have to buy clothes as often.

At school, talk to the principal. You can ask about replacing old toilets and sinks. You can also ask about getting sinks that turn off **automatically**.

Finally, get in touch with your lawmakers. These leaders have the power to make the biggest changes

 Many people attend protests to support protecting freshwater sources.

of all. Ask them to make stronger rules for farms and factories. If everyone does their part, we can reduce water waste.

Using Less Water

Write your answers on a separate piece of paper.

1. Write a paragraph explaining the main ideas of Chapter 2.

2. Do you think your area is doing enough to reduce water waste? Why or why not?

3. Who has the power to make the biggest changes in reducing water waste?
   - **A.** lawmakers
   - **B.** principals
   - **C.** students

4. Which of these actions is most helpful in reducing water waste?
   - **A.** buying clothes that won't last long
   - **B.** taking baths instead of showers
   - **C.** eating more plant-based meals

5. What does **tap** mean in this book?

Many people take long showers. Others keep the tap on while they wash dishes.

   A. a device that controls a faucet

   B. a soft hit against an object

   C. the amount of time needed to
do something

6. What does **survive** mean in this book?

*Instead, they grow native plants. These plants can usually **survive** without being watered. So, there is no need for wasteful sprinklers.*

   A. to waste something

   B. to stay alive

   C. to get wet

Answer key on page 32.

Glossary

automatically
Done on its own, without any outside control.

designers
People who come up with plans for how to make new products.

droughts
Long periods of little or no rain.

evaporates
Changes from liquid to gas.

low-income
Earning little pay.

manager
A person who is in charge of a business.

native
Living or growing naturally in a particular region.

runoff
Water from rain or snow that flows along the ground until it joins a river or stream.

sources
Places where things come from.

To Learn More

BOOKS

Flynn, Riley. *Water Isn't Wasted! How Does Water Become Safe to Drink?* North Mankato, MN: Capstone Press, 2019.

McCarthy, Cecilia Pinto. *Harvesting Fog for Water.* Minneapolis: Abdo Publishing, 2020.

Spalding, Maddie. *The Water Cycle.* Mankato, MN: The Child's World, 2019.

NOTE TO EDUCATORS

Visit **www.focusreaders.com** to find lesson plans, activities, links, and other resources related to this title.

Index

A
aerators, 20

C
cities, 18
clothes, 5, 7, 12, 25–26

D
dishwashers, 6–7
droughts, 12

F
factories, 12, 18, 26–27
farms, 10, 16–17, 27
faucets, 9, 15, 20

L
lawmakers, 26
lawns, 10, 16
leaks, 7, 9, 24

R
rain gardens, 18

S
showers, 5, 7, 9, 23
sinks, 7, 24, 26
sprinklers, 10, 16–17

T
toilets, 15, 26

Answer Key: 1. Answers will vary; **2.** Answers will vary; **3.** A; **4.** C; **5.** A; **6.** B